SPLIT IN TWO

First published in 2009 by
Zest Books, an imprint of Orange Avenue Publishing
35 Stillman Street, Suite 121, San Francisco, CA 94107
www.zestbooks.net

Created and produced by Zest Books, San Francisco, CA
© 2009 by Orange Avenue Publishing LLC
Illustrations © 2009 by Corinne Mucha

Typeset in Garth Graphic, Frutiger, and SF Zero Gravity

Teen Nonfiction / Family / Marriage and Divorce

Library of Congress Control Number: 2008936059

CREDITS
EDITORIAL DIRECTOR: Karen Macklin
CREATIVE DIRECTOR: Hallie Warshaw
ART DIRECTOR: Tanya Napier
WRITER: Karen Buscemi
EDITOR: Karen Macklin
ADDITIONAL RESEARCH AND EDITING: Jeremy Bagai
ILLUSTRATOR: Corinne Mucha
COVER DESIGN: Tanya Napier
DESIGN AND PRODUCTION: Cari McLaughlin
TEEN ADVISORY BOARD: Atticus Graven, Carolyn Hou, Lisa Macklin,
                     Andrea Mufarreh, Trevor Nibbi, Maxfield J. Peterson,
                     Joe Pinsker, Sasha Schmitz, Hannah Shr

Printed in Canada
First printing, 2009
10 9 8 7 6 5 4 3 2 1

*Every effort has been made to ensure that the information presented is
accurate. Readers are strongly advised to read product labels, follow
manufacturers' instructions, and heed warnings. The publisher disclaims
any liability for injuries, losses, untoward results, or any other damages
that may result from the use of the information in this book.*

Using 12,660 lb. of Rolland Enviro100 Book instead
of virgin fibers paper reduces this book's ecological footprint by :

Trees : 108
Solid waste : 3,102kg
Water : 293,408L
Suspended particles in the water : 19.6kg
Air emissions : 6,811kg
Natural gas : 443m3

It's the equivalent of :
Trees : 2.2 football fields
Water : a shower of 13.6 days
Air emissions : emissions of 1.4 cars per year

Recycled
Supporting responsible use
of forest resources
www.fsc.org Cert no. SW-COC-000952
© 1996 Forest Stewardship Council

FSC

Split in Two

Keeping It Together When Your Parents Live Apart

Karen Buscemi

When I was growing up (back in the '80s), my parents were the first ones on my block to split up. I was five, and it was years until I had even one friend in the same situation. Now, having split-up parents is a lot more common. And so are the headaches that come with it.

I don't know about your parents, but mine were very good at telling me and my brother that they still loved us and that the divorce was not our fault. So I got that. But what I never quite understood was how to make my life work while living in two homes. I always left things behind at one place or the other, got confused by the different house rules, and was propelled into a sort of culture shock each time I went from my mom's to my dad's. (Climate shock, too: In the winter, my mom blasted the heat and my dad never even turned it on!)

For a while, my brother and I both lived mostly with my mom and visited my dad on weekends. Then I moved in with my dad, and visited my mom and brother on weekends and at other times during the year. The switching back and forth was a drag. I walked to school, so I needed two different sets of friends to walk with, depending on what neighborhood I was in. I had to carry all my books back and forth to both houses and give everyone all of my home numbers so they could try to locate me (no cell phones back then). And when both of my parents remarried, I had to learn to share my homes with their spouses.

I felt disoriented and unsettled. And while there were lots of books and TV shows encouraging me to talk about my feelings, I just wanted to know where I was going to get lunch money, who would take me back-to-school shopping, who was going to find out if I skipped math class, and which parent would decide whether I could take that part-time job or go on that ski trip.

The point is that—although there still would have been hassles to contend with—scheduling, packing, organizing, and negotiating are all skills that would have helped me a lot. And that's why Zest decided to do this book. We hope it helps you feel more grounded, independent, and sane (and less like disowning your parents, stealing their car, and heading as far east or west as that half-tank of gas will take you).

Karen Macklin,

EDITOR

YOUR PARENTS HAVE SPLIT UP.

And whether or not you understand why they're no longer together, it's important right now to keep your own life on track. After all, the most disrupting thing about your parents' split-up is that it's ... disrupting.

This is a practical guide to help you through the impractical situation of traveling back and forth between two homes. Whether you shuffle between houses every day, once a week, or once a month, the problem remains: You are always in motion. You're stuck in the middle, and your stuff is everywhere. You can't find your textbooks, much less your homework, and the notebook that tells you when your assignments are due is always at the other house. One stepparent treats you like you're five years old, and the

other seems to think you're five years older than you are. Two sets of rules, two sets of responsibilities: one case of confusion.

In this book, you'll learn how to reclaim your sense of self, gain more independence, and keep your head and stuff together. You'll find tips on how to negotiate with your parents to get things you need, as well as how to become a better packer, organizer, money saver, and interior designer. You'll also read tales from others who have gone through the split-living experience and lived to tell the tale. The whole point is to help you feel less crazed and confused, and more self-confident, grounded, and whole: like a sane person living one life, not a scattered person who always feels split in two.

The Daily Shuffle

*Analyzing Your New
(or Not-So-New)
Arrangement*

Your parents have split up, and that means you are trekking back and forth on some sort of regular (or irregular) basis. Living in two houses definitely comes with advantages (two allowances, one-on-one time with a parent, and maybe even more independence), but it also comes with problems—as you probably know all too well already. Do you feel it could all work better than it does?

If so, start by analyzing your present living situation. This way you can see what you've got going for you and what you're up against. See which of the arrangements on the following pages best fits your current situation.

Weekend Visitation

You live with one parent during the week and the other for all or part of the weekend.

Pros

1. It's probably the least disruptive arrangement, at least as far as your social and school life are concerned.

2. You don't need to have two sets of everything — just pack your bags and go.

Cons

1. It's hard to feel at home in a house you visit only on weekends.

2. It may put a real damper on your weekend social life. (Your biggest concern may be scheduling away-time without trampling on your parent's feelings. After all, your dad has been looking forward to Jenga Night with you, while you've been looking forward to some alone time with the girl/guy from biology class.)

>> *I feel like I have no one place to live. My home is always moving, so I never am really at one place.* >>

DANI, 16

Every Other Day

You're at your mom's house one night, then Dad's, then Mom's, etc.

Pros

1. If you really like being around both parents, this is the best arrangement: You are only away one day at a time.

2. The constant moving back and forth means you'll need a decent mode of transportation. And that line of thinking could even land you your own car. Maybe.

Cons

1. Every day is moving day, and moving takes time and energy. You and your parents all need to be on the ball.

2. You really do need two sets of most things; otherwise you are literally living out of a backpack.

> ❰❰ *I am glad I get to see both of my parents. I have friends whose parents are divorced and they never stayed in contact with one of their parents.* ❱❱

KIM, 14

The Split Week

You live the first half of the week at one house, the second half at the other. This means you'll spend some school days plus part of the weekend at each house.

Pros

1. This arrangement is a little less chaotic than moving every single day; staying a few nights at each place means less packing.

2. Again, you get to see both parents equal amounts, which is cool if you like them both.

Cons

1. You only have one weekend day (and night!) at each place, so your social life might get confusing.

2. Unless your parents are really organized, this can be a more chaotic arrangement; both parents may forget who is supposed to be doing what and when.

> « *To make transitions easier, make sure you do one thing consistently at each house. Every time I switch houses, my dad and I do a night-time grocery store run and race our shopping carts. I always know that will be a constant when I switch to my dad's house.* »
>
> SOPHIE, 17

Alternate Weeks

You live at one house for an entire week and then switch.

Pros

1. You may feel calmer if you move around less, and you'll probably find it easier to remember to haul must-haves back and forth.

2. You actually get to spend big chunks of time with each parent, which can be nice for bonding purposes—plus you have enough time away from each one to actually miss them!

Cons

1. You might also be away from a favorite pet or your best neighborhood friend, making you feel homesick or just plain out of touch.

2. Again, you definitely need two of most things, one at each house. You may be able to live without your Xbox for a night or two, but for a whole week?

« *Because of the separation, it's easier to have good one-on-one relationships with your parents.* »

NADJA, 15

«Living in two homes is hard. You have to have enough stuff at each house, and getting to the other parent's house is time-consuming. It's also hard when you miss a parent while you're at the other parent's house, and it's difficult to have to split your time between your parents and your friends.»

AMANDA, 16

Summers and Holidays

You have a parent living in another state (or country) whom you only get to stay with at certain times of the year.

Pros

1. Being with that parent always feels like vacation.

2. It's nice to change scenery and get away for long stretches of time.

Cons

1. You give up a lot of your social life (you have to watch your friends make summer plans, knowing you won't be around to take part in the pool parties and camping trips).

2. The out-of-town parent's house and neighborhood is like a foreign land, with no social outings (dinner with Aunt Ruth does *not* count) to fill your days.

« I don't get to hang out with my friends as much as I did before because my dad lives far away. »

ZOLA, 14

What Now?

Does your living arrangement resemble any of those just described? Or do you have a whole different situation? If so, take a minute to figure out its pros and cons. You've probably heard this before, but knowing what you're up against is half the battle.

It's great to know what *is* working for you, and to acknowledge that. But it's also important to learn how to talk to your parents about what's *not* working for you. Next stop: Negotiating.

« There is no time limit on how long it takes one to cope. There is not an exact timetable for everyone; people react differently to hard things in life. »

SOPHIE, 17

The Family Bargaining Table

Learning How to Get What You Need

Throughout this book, you'll be identifying things in your living situation that need changing, and figuring out how to change them. But you won't be able to change much on your own. You are part of a family unit (even if it is not a typical nuclear family), and any small or large change you want to make will have to be approved and maybe even carried out by your parents. So what does this mean? You need to learn how to negotiate.

Negotiation isn't reserved for business suits and boardrooms—it's something you do every single day. When your friends want to go out for pizza (again?!), and you agree as long as they pick a restaurant where you can get a salad, you've had a negotiation. Studying with your best friend can be another chance to negotiate. If he's worried about the next day's algebra test, while you're wound up over a chemistry exam, you can suggest taking turns at quizzing each other for 15 minutes. That way, you both get a handle on your respective material.

Your life at home is no different. If you want something, you need to know how to ask for it—and what you're willing to give up in order to get it.

10 Golden Rules of Negotiation

Lots of people are afraid of negotiating. They think: What if I ask for too much? What if I don't ask for enough? What if I piss off my parents and then get grounded? But negotiation is less scary if you think of it as a game you can learn to play. Large stakes or small, the same rules apply.

1. Organize and prioritize your goals

Before coming to your parents with an issue, you'll need to do your homework. Half the skill in negotiating is preparation. To start, think about what you are asking for and what you are willing to concede. Let's say you want more privacy at your mom's house, so you ask if you can move into the den, which is twice the size of

your bedroom and gets very dusty. Are you willing to dust and vacuum your new room in exchange for the switch?

Or maybe you feel like you are always broke by the time the weekend comes. Are you willing to do some extra chores to get more money? And will you ask for an increased allowance or just cash for one special item? Determine these things before you enter the ring.

2. Be specific and ask for what you actually need

Say you've decided that your present curfew at Dad's house is way too early and needs to be 11, as it is at Mom's house. Now ask yourself why. Do you want to spend more time at a friend's house? Need an extra hour to take the bus home from night practices?

If you start out with "I need a later curfew because Mom gives me one," you are likely to get a flat-out denial or an arbitrary compromise ("Eleven is too late, but I'm willing to try 8:30"). However, if you communicate the reasons behind your request, you may get a different solution that also works (your parents will agree to let you have friends over until 11, or they'll pick you up at 10 and save you a bus or cab ride home).

Just make sure you are honest about your needs. If you want that extended curfew because you'd like to stay later at your boyfriend's or girlfriend's house, but say that you need it so that you can study late with a friend, your parent may suggest having the friend over to your house. Oops.

3. Identify your parents' interests

You may know what YOU need, but do you know what
your parents need? Have you asked? If you do a little
investigating, you may not only see that your mom's
and/or dad's concerns are valid — you may also come
up with a solution that works for everyone.

Let's say again that you want your curfew at 11; your
dad wants it at 8:30. Rather than compromise at 9:30
or trade hours for extra chores, discuss the concerns
behind the stances. If your dad is just concerned for
your safety (likely), then maybe checking in by
phone every hour after 8 p.m. and filling him in
on exactly who you'll be with will do the trick.

4. Do some research

You've decided you need a new cell phone/automobile/
spaceship, and you can articulate why (stay in touch
with friends/be less dependent on parents to shuttle you
back and forth/really need to get away from everyone).
That's a great start, but you know your parents will ask
for more info than that. How much will it cost? How
will you (or they!) pay for it? What are the legal require-
ments? Do some basic research and consider writing up
a document for everyone to look at during your meeting. The more information you can show up with, the
better your argument will be. Plus, your parents will
appreciate your maturity.

5. Consider where and when to meet

Put some thought into the best setting for your conversation. A quick appeal as you're rushing out the door for school might be fine if the issue is a request for a few bucks to help you buy a burrito that day, but not if the issue is getting a lock on your door to keep a new five-year-old stepsister out. The more important the topic, the more you'll want to schedule a time and place where people can be focused. But for less difficult issues, feel free to move away from the formal bargaining table. Relaxed conversations often occur during some other activity, like cooking, fishing, museum strolling, or chilling at the baseball game.

6. Decide who needs to be there

Think about who is involved. Want to borrow the car
for a date Friday night? You can probably work that
out with Mom or Dad alone. But what if you and your
stepbrother both have dates, both want to borrow the
car, and the idea of a double date isn't thrilling either of
you. Or maybe you've found a summer camp you'd like
to attend, or a summer job you'd like to take — far away
from both parents' homes. In situations like this, you
need to gather a group.

It may seem daunting to have a whole-family
meeting that involves stepparents and siblings
(or even both of your split-up parents), but bringing

everyone together to face a problem can have great results. You'll find that there are more perspectives in the room to drive creative problem solving, and no one feels slighted or singled out as the enemy because they weren't part of the conversation.

7. Listen

One of the most important elements of negotiating is listening. That doesn't mean doing the "I sort of hear you but I'm busy forming a response in my head" thing. That means *really* hearing what others have to say. Give your full attention to the person who has the floor and ask the group to do the same. This makes the people included in your discussion feel that you care what they are saying; in turn, this makes them more receptive to your thoughts. Listening well will also give you insight into what will set off your audience and what will pull them into your corner. And you may even come to see where the other people in your family are coming from.

8. Be partners, not opponents

The biggest mistake a person can make when negotiating is one of attitude: Instead of considering the other parties as opponents, think of them as partners in a group venture. (Which, strangely enough, is actually what they are.) Together, your goal is to find win-win solutions that make everyone happy — at least most of the time.

» *Work as a team with your parents. Doing this will allow you to learn with them as well as from them. I was angry with both of my parents for a long time for getting divorced. I thought it was selfish of them. But that only made matters worse. They needed my support and love, too. As I grew, I forgave my parents and felt extremely proud of them for overcoming an obstacle as large as divorce.* »

JEFF, 24

9. Stay calm

OK, you presented your case well, you heard the other party's concerns, you used all of your best negotiation skills, and you still got an "I'll think about it." Whatever you do, don't lose your temper. That will only ruin your chances.

> ◀◀ *You need to really take care of yourself and make sure that you tell your parents how the separation is affecting you.* ▶▶
>
> NADJA, 15

Instead, realize that an "I'll think about it" is actually a good sign — it's not a "no"! Also, accept that you will not always get an immediate yes, no, or counteroffer. Don't expect to settle every matter with one discussion. Instead, expect to talk again, and stay calm and focused. Your parents want to feel as though they are making the best decision possible; let them ask questions and, if need be, sleep on it.

10. Be yourself

Whatever your negotiation, don't go in trying to be as tough as a *CSI* detective. Speak from the heart, be yourself, and let your winning personality shine through. Your parents will respond more positively to lovable you than to anything dramatic, cutesy, or manipulative.

In the end, it's important to remember that you may not end up with everything you want. Some things you might get, but not in the time frame you'd prefer. And sometimes the answer really will be "no." For now. But your living situation will always be changing, and so will your parents' feelings as you get older. If you didn't get what you wanted today, don't think it was all for naught. Some things take time, like chipping away at a big rock. Your negotiation today may have just laid the groundwork for a different one in six months. Or even six weeks. So, above all, have the conversation!

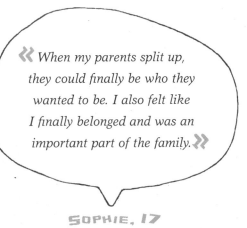

When my parents split up, they could finally be who they wanted to be. I also felt like I finally belonged and was an important part of the family.

SOPHIE, 17

BEST (& WORST)

Split-in-Two Moments

KIM, 14

My dad was driving me to my mom's home an hour earlier than usual so I could go to youth group. I was very thankful to him, because I knew he was giving up an hour of our time together to get me there. Then my mom called my cell phone while my dad and I were in the car and asked if I wanted to go to this haunted firehouse that night instead. It was a place my cousins and I would go every year, and that was the last night it was open.

I really wanted to go, but my dad got really mad that I was going to blow off youth group after he had gone out of his way to take me back to my mom's early. I went to the haunted house and I had a lot of fun, but felt bad for blowing off my dad. I later apologized to him, and he accepted my apology and said that he would continue to get me to youth group on time.

Your Room — and Your Other Room

Making It Feel Like Home in Both Houses

One of the most basic things that your split-home lifestyle can disrupt is your ability to feel at home. Before, you had one room; now you have two. And in this instance, two is not always better than one.

If you take a look at both rooms, it's likely that only one of them actually feels like home. That room is filled with all your stuff, while the other one is either stark as a summer camp tent or decorated by a parent (or stepparent) who clearly appreciates a different color scheme than you do.

If you want to feel comfortable in both houses (and that's a necessity if you want to keep your sanity), you need to like (even love) your living quarters. Don't fall into the trap of thinking the rooms have to be similar—they don't. See this as an opportunity to express yourself twice. One environment can be playful, the other serene. Or one may be cheerfully bright, and the other film-noir. Experiment with different décor, different colors, and different lighting. If you treat this situation like an interior design project, you can actually have fun with it.

❮❮ *The biggest disadvantage to living in two houses was lacking a sense of home. My mind and body had to adapt to two places while I yearned for one home base. It sort of felt like camping or hotel-hopping at first. I didn't have one bed. I didn't have one room. I even had two toothpastes. Each house had different soaps, different foods, different rules, different everything.* ❯❯

JEFF, 24

The Basics

A bed, nightstand, and a dresser is not a bedroom — it's a hotel room. Transforming that space into one that makes you feel comfortable will take some time and energy. If you are moving into a new room, start with the nonnegotiables:

Do you have a comfy bed and enough blankets?

Is the temperature suitable for humans throughout the night? Throughout the day?

Do you have a door, or at least line-of-sight privacy?

Do you have a quiet place to read/relax/do homework?

Do you have the basic furniture you need?

Any unresolved issues on this list demand attention from you and your family as soon as possible. Once those are all settled, it's time to explore some more personal options—making sure your music system is set up the way you like it, for example, or that you have the right nightstand lamp so that you can read in bed before going to sleep.

The Layout and Look

Where you place furniture and accessories can play a major role in how happy you are in your room, and even in how well you sleep. So can color and light. If you need help deciding how to lay stuff out, you can google "feng shui" (a traditional Chinese practice of creating good energy by arranging objects in harmony) or simply "interior design" to get some ideas. Use the negotiation skills from Chapter 2 to ask your parents for permission and for help changing things up. And remember: There are lots of great low-budget ways to redesign a room. Always look at garage sales, used furniture stores, and discount department stores when shopping for stuff for your room.

Consider these tips when planning your rooms:

1. Your bed

Position your bed where it works best for you. Do you love to dance in your bedroom? Place the bed in a corner so you have the most floor space possible. Are you a video game junkie? Moving the bed so that it's sideways to the TV allows plenty of room for you and a friend to sit on the floor, prop pillows, and lean back against the bed while you play. Do you prefer symmetry and a room that has a more stylized feel? Place the bed at the middle of a wall and add bedside tables on both sides, with an alarm clock on one and a lamp on the other.

« You should divide the things you are really fond of between both rooms so they both feel like home. Otherwise, you may end up loving one room and utterly hating the other. »

WESLEY, 15

« At first, I slept on a futon and lived out of boxes at my dad's house. I also lived in hotels, as well as in several rental houses. Nothing was ever consistent, which is the only thing I really wanted, so it was difficult. »

SOPHIE, 17

2. Your décor

Art is a great way to express your personality and make your room feel more you. Whether you're into black-and-white movie posters or everything Hello Kitty, get some inexpensive posters, pottery, sculpture, and calendars to make your room feel fun and finished. Place the art or poster you like best on the wall opposite your bed so that it's the first thing you see each morning.

3. The lighting

That harsh ceiling light is great if you've lost an earring or safety pin in your carpet. Otherwise, have at least one other light in your room that is softer and more relaxing. The easiest option is a small lamp on a bedside table, preferably with a low wattage. (But not so low that you need a flashlight to read.)

4. The colors

Color affects your mood more than anything else, so it's so important to choose hues that you like. You may not be allowed to paint your room any color you want (though it is always worth asking), but make sure your room-accents (bedsheets, pillows, beanbag chairs, etc.) are in colors you gel with. Do you like nature? Go with greens, browns, and cream colors. Want your room to feel soothing? Go for a variation of blue hues. Like things a little loud? Add punches of color in orange or violet with an accent pillow, a piece of art, or a lampshade.

One bonus to having two houses is that I have two rooms and I get double the stuff.

TRAVERS, 17

Yours, Mine, and Ours

Not enough bedrooms to go around? If you have no choice but to share, never fear. You can bunk with a sibling and still make your room feel like you.

Your negotiation skills will again be helpful here. To start, have a sit-down with your roomie and decide on a design theme you both like. Keep an open mind about different ideas and how you can incorporate your personality into the décor. For example, say you want every inch of the room dripping in pink, but your sister is set on a sports theme, which doesn't inspire you at all. You can compromise on a beach theme, where your sister gets elements of boogie boarding and beach volleyball, while you can add big (pink!) sunglasses, a beach umbrella, and bikini-printed pillows. If you guys get along well enough, this can be a great opportunity for artistic collaboration.

The other option is to have a clear separation of sides. You decorate your side the way you like, while your sibling decorates the other side his/her own way. This can often work out fine as long as you come to agreements on who gets what wall space, floor space, and closet space. When in doubt, measure things to be 50–50. Maybe even hang up a beaded, bamboo, or fabric curtain that can be closed if either of you wants privacy. Remember, you're going to be spending a lot of time together in this room, so start off on a positive note, working together and being flexible enough to make a change or two so you're both happy with your finished space. When you go to college and are forced to share a room with a roommate you don't know, you'll be an expert in how to make it work.

Staking Out Your Territory

Let's face it: You never want people wandering into your room uninvited and riffling through your stuff. And while that may not have been a problem before, everything changes if and when you add new stepparents and siblings into the mix. If you find yourself sharing a home with new people, use your communication and negotiation skills and call a family meeting to discuss privacy and respect for each other's things. Be sure to cover the differences between asking and assuming, borrowing and browsing. Get everyone involved in making some ground rules so no one feels picked on. This process isn't foolproof, but it's a good way to start.

If you're sharing a room, you need to arrange times of the day when you can be assured alone time to relax, do homework, or talk on the phone. For example, on weekdays from 5-6 p.m., you get your room to yourself while your roommate gets it from 6-7 p.m.

Remember that your room is more than just a space. It's a big component of your state of mind. If you like where you live and sleep, you've won half the battle.

I'm Supposed to Be Where When?

Dealing with Your Crazy Schedule

Sure, everyone has a crazy schedule these days. But navigating a busy itinerary is harder to do when your time is split between two houses— especially if one is some distance from your school, your friends, or your job. Not knowing where you are supposed to be and when is completely stressful, for both you and your parents. It can also make you feel really scattered.

Getting organized may sound less than exciting, but it's true what people say: With structure comes freedom. Once you have a system in place, you'll be less consumed with the minute-to-minute chaos of your life, and more able to concentrate on important things—like school, that new crush, or how to win the championship game. Organization also equals more independence. For one thing, you can schedule your time better if you actually know what your weeks—and your parents' weeks—look like in advance. This will also help you figure out ways to get from place A to place B more easily.

With the right tools and skills, and a little practice, you may soon be even more organized than your parents.

> ❮❮ *Living in two homes makes organizing school stuff extremely difficult. I often have to make trips back and forth from my mom's house to my dad's house on weekdays just to grab a folder or something, and I realize that's not even possible for a lot of kids. I think it has impacted my grades several times, and I haven't figured out how to balance it all out.* ❯❯

MAX, 16

Choosing a Calendar System

First things first: You need a calendar. There's just too much stuff going on to keep track of it all in your (or your parent's) head—and forgetting about a softball game, concert, or field trip can necessitate a 6 a.m. emergency trip to your other house for your stuff. A good calendar system will ensure you have the things you need for the next day, the next week, and even the next month.

Decide on the calendar that works best for your situation and keep your important dates front and center. There are three basic types of scheduling devices you can use to keep track of yourself (and your parents). You may find that you need only one, or a combination of two or three.

1. Internet calendar

If you have easy Internet access at both houses, using some type of Web-based planner is probably the best method for keeping track of schedules for both you and your parents. There are many Web-based calendars out there (Google, Yahoo, Microsoft), and most of them are free. This is an amazingly easy way to keep track of who's taking you to the dentist, who's chaperoning your school dance (which you now may want to skip), and who's picking you up from rehearsal.

The bonuses to using an online calendar:
1. It can be shared between all three of you (as well as any siblings and stepparents who are in the mix). That

means you and your parents can add or edit events as needed, without the need for phone tag, voicemails, or sticky notes. (This method also turns out to be extremely helpful if Mom and Dad aren't communicating well off-line.) For extra clarity (and flair), use a different color for each person's schedule.

2. You don't need to have an online calendar with you. You can access it from any computer anywhere.

3. You can use an online calendar to remind yourself about stuff. Send notes to yourself: "Remember to pack uniform for Sunday's game" or "Don't forget to e-mail Dad the school picture payment info." With some programs, you can even send those reminders to your e-mail or cell phone or PDA.

4. You can be as public or private as you want. Share only parts of the calendar and keep your own stuff private. This is great when you want your parents to see where to pick you up on Thursday, but not the phone number of the guy/girl you promised to call on Friday.

To find the best Internet calendar for you, do an online search, check out what each has to offer, and select one that suits your needs. Then prepare yourself for the real challenge: teaching your parents how to use it. If they are computer savvy, you're golden. If not, plan a few 15-minute tutoring sessions. Short learning sessions generally work better than long ones in which your parents stare at the computer screen quizzically in between yawns. If you write down a step-by-step list of what to do, your folks will be especially grateful.

2. Jumbo wall calendar

If your parents are not technologically savvy, or just generally like to have things right in front of their faces to help remind them of stuff, a large paper or dry-erase calendar is a great option.

The bonuses to using a jumbo calendar:
1. It's available at all times, even when your computer is off. You, your mom, or your dad can write something on it right after walking in the door, and you can leave them reminder notes to feed your fish while you are gone.

2. A wall calendar serves as a constant reminder. Every time you walk into the kitchen, living room, or wherever you've decided to hang it, you can't help but see it. If something only lives on your Internet calendar, you have to actually remember to check it; with a wall calendar, you can't miss it.

Coordinating Mom's and Dad's wall calendars is the only tricky part here, otherwise you'll end up with calendar chaos. Keep them both updated or have a Web-based calendar and/or your own portable planner as backup.

« Living in two homes is really hard in any situation. It is important to take a big deep breath and organize yourself. »

DANI, 16

3. Portable planner

This method is great for people who like to have their schedule with them all the time. It's also a great supplement to both a jumbo calendar and an Internet calendar. PDAs and some cell phones can serve as personal planners, but keep in mind that they can run out of battery or crash—things that paper planners won't do.

The bonuses to using a portable planner:
1. It's portable. Plain and simple. You can toss it in your backpack or handbag, and write info down the moment you find out about it, whether you're online or not.

2. It's personal. It's for your eyes only. You can keep all of your private stuff in here (social, academic, or what have you), and just transcribe the stuff your parents need to know onto the Internet calendar or jumbo calendar when you get home each day.

No matter what kind of planner(s) you choose, make sure that you and your parents come up with a system for maintaining them. Do your best to make sure that all pertinent info is getting to all of the parties involved. Every family is different, so figure out what works best with your folks.

What Gets Written Down

Once you have your calendar system, you'll need to figure out what actually goes onto the calendar. Here are three general categories to consider.

1. Basic events

This is the everyday, regular stuff, all of which needs to go on the calendar: practices and games, work, appointments, study groups, parties, vacations, concerts, mall trips, and family events. Also, ask your parents to add everything they have going on that might affect your schedule.

2. Transportation

You know where you want to be, but how will you get there? Is a parent willing to drive you? Can you borrow a car? Or do you need to find another way (friend, bus, bike, tractor)? Make sure you note transportation arrangements on your calendar, and get the relevant parties to sign off their approval. You don't want to find yourself stranded when you're supposed to be at the front row of a concert.

3. Parental play time

It might not seem like a big deal to you to ditch your mom on Scrabble Night for a friend's party, but she may have spent the last week memorizing words that start with "X" for her big evening with you. If your parents want to spend time with you, take them up on it! To prevent parental time from impeding your social life, schedule time with them on the calendar — and not on nights when you have a hot date or a big party.

❮ My family and I keep a planner that has all the things I need to do, which house I will be at, and who will be picking me up. That way we can all stay on the same page. ❯

WESLEY, 15

Managing Your Time

In a life full of schoolwork, homework, sports, artistic pursuits, a social life, and familial obligations, it's difficult enough for anyone to manage his or her time. But if you live in a split-family situation, your familial obligations can feel like they are doubled or tripled. For one thing, both of your parents see you less than they did before, so when you are around they want to spend more of that time with you. In addition, you now need to factor in separate time to spend with your mom's family/friends/new romantic partner and your dad's family/friends/new romantic partner. It's kind of like having in-laws, except that you are nowhere close to being married.

This is why you probably feel at times that everyone wants a piece of you — and that you are not free to have a life of your own. Maybe your mom really wants you to hang out with her and her new boyfriend this Saturday. Then your dad says he wants to take you to meet his new wife's family out in the country on Sunday. Uh, great, but what happened to your weekend?

With all these demands, it's important to manage — and protect — your own time. That means doing your best to see all of the people your parents want you to see and also knowing when to ask for a "get out of jail free" card (which may actually be a "get out of dinner with your stepparent's sister-in-law's roommate free" card). Instead of miserably agreeing to all demands — or always retorting with a flat-out "no" — have a discussion with your parents about how much family time they can each reasonably expect of you. Remind them that you're now dividing your total family time between two sides of the family, so each side will only get about half that total. This negotiation, by the way, will continue with your family well past high school.

> ❮❮ *It can be very hard to plan my time because I always have to take into account which house I will be going to or coming from and how much time it will take. It can sometimes be quite annoying when I realize I won't be able to do something because I can't make it home in time.* ❯❯
>
> WESLEY, 15

Dividing Special Occasion Time

Having split-up parents gets more complicated around special occasions. Mom and Dad could both have plans for you that you might not even know about until the last minute, when you discover you're double-booked. Here are some suggestions for dealing with holiday, birthday, and vacation madness.

1. Holidays

In split families, celebration navigation becomes an art. How holidays are handled will depend on how many people are hosting, the timing of the events, and where houses are located. For example, if your dad's Uncle Lenny is having Thanksgiving on his farm at 3:30 p.m, and your mom's Aunt Tootsie is planning a similar feast at her condo in the city at 4, there's obviously no way you're going to make it to both events (and your stomach may thank you for that). Chances are, your parents will decide which event you're attending, so if you were looking forward to feeding the chickens at the farm, you'll need to speak up.

However, if one side of the family is sitting down for a meal in the early afternoon, while the other is breaking bread in the evening, you can realistically plan to spend the holiday with both parents. Just make it clear that Grandma shouldn't feel slighted if you've already eaten an entire bird at the earlier dinner and don't want to indulge a second time. Nobody has to gain ten pounds trying to please everybody.

As you can imagine, sorting all of this out takes some negotiation between your parents (help them out with what you read in Chapter 2). In some families, Mom's (or Dad's) side will agree to have Thanksgiving (or Hanukkah, Christmas, or whatever) a day later, in order to accommodate everyone's schedules. In the end, the holidays are more about being together than celebrating on an exact date. If your parents lose sight of that, don't hesitate to remind them.

2. Birthdays

For birthdays, you have a few options. One parent takes the day, the other takes the evening. Or maybe one parent takes Saturday, and the other, Sunday. Or maybe you hang out with your friends instead. It's your birthday, so it's really up to you. Of course, this is also a great opportunity to stretch your birthday into a birth-week and have three or four times as many celebrations as you would normally have—if your family goes in for that sort of thing.

> *The best part of my parents' splitting up was having two of everything. Christmases, birthdays, beds, closets. And then I eventually got two new stepparents who have been a major influence in my life.*

KELSEY, 19

« *In my parents' early years of divorce my dad would come to my mom's house and we would still all get together for Christmas and Thanksgiving. But when my dad met another special someone, that all changed. We had to plan two Christmases and two Thanksgivings. I thought that moving away for college would help, but it did the exact opposite. When I would come home for the weekend, I had to make a complete schedule for which houses I would stay at and when, bouncing around all weekend to see everybody. I couldn't just relax and go with the flow.* »

JEFF, 24

« *I hate having to go back and forth on the same day on holidays to spend time with both parents.* »

AMANDA, 16

3. Vacation

Vacation scheduling generally creates fewer conflicts, unless both parents want to whisk you away for spring break, which is unlikely. Now that you have a calendar system that works, use it to ensure that your family getaways don't interfere with each other or with some social event you were planning to attend. If there is a schedule conflict, talk to your parents about it calmly. It's hard to be excited about a trip when you know that you're missing out on something else big.

> ❮❮ *If you're at your mom's house, sometimes you miss something that happens that weekend with your friends because you are hanging out with your mom.* ❯❯

AMANDA, 16

Whatever your preferences for holidays, birthdays, and vacations, be sure to voice your opinions far enough in advance that your choices can be worked into each family's plan. Nobody will know what you want unless you speak up.

And when talking about a vacation with your parent, consider this: It could be fun to plan a short getaway for just the two of you. Big family vacations with siblings, new stepfamily, or a parent's significant other can be fun, but it's important to keep close bonds with your parents, too. Invite your mom or dad on a trip to see your favorite football team play in another city, a hiking trip in the woods, or a theater or spa weekend in the city. Now that your parents are no longer a unit, you may get to know them on a whole different level than you would have if they had stayed married.

One of the advantages to having your parents split up is that you start to notice the distinct personality of each parent, whereas when they're together, their personalities may blend. Now you have a really separate relationship with each parent, so your mom's or dad's unique style and way of life is more apparent—and you can bond with that side of them.

JOSH, 20

The Life of an Intrepid Traveler

Learning How to Pack and Haul It All

If you're living in two homes, you are probably becoming the queen or king of packing. It can be a complete drag at times, especially when you forget things (like homework or a favorite book or game) at the other house. Constant re-packing can also make you feel pretty scattered, unsettled, and even exhausted.

But there is an art to packing and hauling stuff, and knowing that art can help you go from feeling like a homeless vagabond to an intrepid traveler. A good packing system can help you pack efficiently and quickly, and also help keep your breakables safe, your clothes only semi-wrinkled, and your stuff more or less condensed and portable. Knowing what and how to pack is a skill you will use your entire life, making you a better, more easygoing, and more flexible traveler.

BEST
(& WORST)
Split-in-Two Moments

BEN, 17

Once I was having a sleepover at my dad's house and, like every good sleepover, it needed an Xbox, which was (not so conveniently) at my mom's. I left a pleading message on her phone to please bring it over, but when she didn't reply for half an hour my phone died and my friend and I bused over to her house. By the time we got there, she had received our message and had driven the box over to my dad's house, leaving us to take the 45-minute trip back again. After that we were so exhausted we barely played any video games at all.

10 Tips to Help You Get Your Packing Act Together

1. List it

Before you start packing, create a packing list. This will save you from the agony of discovering you left behind a beloved concert T-shirt or favorite squishy pillow. Take your time putting this list together, so when you begin to pack, you don't randomly toss "I might need these" items into your bag and forget the "Dang, I should have packed those" items altogether. Don't forget to include the ever-important chargers for your phone, laptop, iPod, and camera! Check off the items on the list as you place them in your bag, and save the list somewhere that will be easy to access—in your journal or on your laptop—no matter where you are.

> ❰❰ *Make sure you have the necessities at both houses. I used to have a checklist that I would refer to so I could make sure I had my homework and clothes and stuff ... One time I forgot my computer power cord at my dad's, so I could not use my computer for a week.* ❱❱

TRAVERS, 17

2. Lighten up

The less you pack, the easier your trips back and forth will feel. The easiest way to pack fewer clothes is to stick to a small color palette so everything matches. Also, select clothes that layer well, so you don't always need to bring bulky jackets, and pack minibottles of your toiletries and cosmetics instead of dragging super-sized shampoo or shaving cream bottles back and forth. (Or just have two sets of toiletries, one for each house.) Keep your schoolbooks in a separate backpack so they don't squish your clothing.

3. Think small

Buying something for yourself? If it's something you will want to bring with you when you change houses, consider going with the most compact model or with gadgets that serve more than one purpose. For instance, a laptop with a built-in DVD player eliminates the need to drag around a portable DVD player. Also, a thinner, smaller laptop is easier to haul around than a big clunky one. Anything that lightens your load will make shuffling between houses a more pleasant experience.

4. Avoid wrinkles

Rolling your clothes tightly can save on room *and* on wrinkling. For pants, fold in half lengthwise, then roll. For shirts, fold back the sleeves and then roll. Remember, less folding equals less wrinkling.

> ❮❮ *It seems like, no matter what, all my boxers end up over at one house, and all my socks at the other. There's really no way I can think to control this, especially because the structure of what night I stay at what house is not stabilized and it all becomes really sporadic.* ❯❯

MAX, 16

5. Make space

Consider using packing folders or compression bags (available at most travel-gear stores and Web sites); both let you compact your clothing so it takes up less space. This is especially useful when you visit one parent for a month or longer.

6. Create order

When using a suitcase, pack bulkier clothing items at
the bottom, with the most delicate clothing on top, and
make sure breakable items are cushioned by sweaters
or fuzzy pajamas somewhere in the middle. If you're
using a backpack, place softer, lighter items on the
bottom and put the heavier items, including toiletries,
on top. (Putting heavier items higher up on your back
and closer to your body decreases the chance of lower
back strain.)

*« Always make sure you have
everything you need before
switching homes. Sometimes I
leave my phone charger, homework, retainers, or uniform
shoes at one house, and neither
parent is willing to get it. »*

DANI, 16

7. Use shoes

Place underwear and socks (and any other small objects) inside shoes to save room. Pack shoes by either facing the tops of them toward each other heel to toe, which creates a rectangular base you can stack other items on, or by placing them around the border of your suitcase.

8. Stay dry

Put as many liquid toiletries as possible into small travel containers. Sets of these containers are easy to find at a drugstore; the kind made for air travel is especially good, even if you are only ground traveling. Keep these containers in a closed toiletry bag so you don't wind up with hair gel in your boots. (Ick.) Stock up on zip-lock bags and use them!

9. Stay organized

Keep things separated either by compartment or by when you will need them (things you need sooner go on top). To keep your smaller items separated and easy to find, use travel organizers, such as a jewelry portfolio (available at most travel stores) or zip-lock bags. Have a separate backpack for your school stuff, and always double-check to make sure you've got everything you need before you leave the house.

10. Leave a little extra space

It's possible you'll return with more than you left with. Just one shopping trip can push your suitcase to its limit. Either leave enough room in your luggage for new items, or pack a collapsible bag that can turn into back-pack number two if you need it.

The Bag You Drag

You'll need a proper bag (or bags!) for items you will be hauling between houses. A backpack is great if you switch houses every other night. If you take a laptop back and forth, get a backpack with a built-in laptop case. Longer-term haulers might want to opt for something with wheels, especially if your stuff feels heavy, or a duffel bag if you want something you can swing over your shoulder and carry easily up and down stairs. If one bag feels too heavy, divide your stuff between two smaller ones; they'll wedge more easily into Mom's or Dad's car—and be easier to heave in and out.

Make sure you get doubles of your favorite jeans so you can have those staples at each house.

SOPHIE, 17

Make Yourself Comfortable

Once you get home (whichever home that is), take a
few minutes to unpack. It may be tempting to live
out of your bag or suitcase, especially if you'll be there
for only a few days. However, having your things in
drawers and your clothes in the closet will make you
feel more at home and less like a hotel guest. It will
also help you find your stuff more easily and without
making a mess. And don't forget to reuse that packing
list when it's time to pull all your things together again.
After a while, you'll notice that packing becomes
second nature.

*❮❮ It's important to unpack my stuff,
because it helps me be more
organized and it also helps my
room feel more like home. ❯❯*

WESLEY, 15

BEST

(& WORST)

Split-in-Two Moments

AMANDA, 16

My dad lives about 30 minutes away from my mom's house, which is where I mostly live, but every other weekend I go to my dad's house. One weekend, I brought my tennis shoes to my dad's—a red pair and a black pair—so I could leave one pair there permanently. On Sunday night, when I was leaving my dad's house, I packed my shoes. When I was getting dressed Monday morning at my mom's house, I put on my shoes—but I didn't realize until I got to school that I was wearing one red shoe and one black shoe. I had mixed them up.

Cash Control

*Creating Some
Financial Independence*

One way to feel more in control of your split-in-two life is to exercise some control over your finances. For many kids in split families, the equation is simple: Money equals freedom. Freedom to buy those things that both of your parents keep saying the other one should buy you; freedom to go out on the weekend or get that new pair of jeans despite the fact that your parents are feeling strapped from the costs of the divorce (or even from the costs of a new marriage); freedom to travel (by bus, taxi, or even your own car) back and forth between your friends' houses and parents' houses without always having to rely on them for rides.

Obviously, money comes from a finite number of places: a part-time job, doing odd jobs around your neighborhood, an allowance based on a certain amount of chores, and gifts from relatives. Carefully explore all of your options and start saving ASAP.

Getting a Job

If you're big into sports or involved with some other activity that takes up most of your after-school time, it may be hard to find room in your life for a job. But if you can make the time, earning an income can be liberating. The legal working age differs from state to state. Generally it's 16, although you may be able to get a work permit at 15. Call your local employment office to find out for sure. If you are under 15, there are still plenty of off-the-books jobs you can do. Everybody loves a bargain, and an eager teen offering reasonably-priced services will often get a resounding "yes!" from neighbors too busy, too old, or too lazy to do the work themselves. Consider jobs such as mowing lawns, raking leaves, washing cars, walking dogs, shoveling snow, and babysitting (just make sure you know and trust the people you are working for). And don't forget, having two sets of households gives you two neighborhoods to capitalize on.

Doing Chores for Allowance

If you are not already receiving an allowance based on chores, propose this plan to your parents. You don't need transportation to do chores around the house, and it's a good way to earn extra money. All parents are thrilled to have help at home; they may secretly wish their kids would volunteer the work out of sheer love and adoration, but in reality, they're often willing to pay for the assistance. And once again, two households equals two allowances. Cha-ching!

> *If you can get it to work, each parent will give you an allowance—equaling double the money and double the fun.*

MAX, 16

You don't have to take out the garbage or vacuum the living room to score a few extra dollars — though those things are always needed. You can also be creative about what tasks you offer to take on. For instance, if one parent is an elementary school teacher, you can offer to help grade some spelling tests. If another parent is a carpenter, offer to help with woodcutting, cleanup, or even simple bookkeeping. Make a list of what you could do around the house to generate some cash, and present it to your parents.

❮❮ *A couple of years after my parents split up, I decided I needed some money. So I skillfully stated to both of them that I needed to start getting an allowance. I agreed to do some weekly chores around both houses and so I got two allowances. Neither parent gave me a full load of chores because I was only at each house half of the time, but they both gave me a full allowance! So I was getting two allowances for the work of one!* ❯❯

JOSH, 20

When negotiating your weekly allowances, start with a higher number (within reason) than you think you can get. This way, you have wiggle room if your parents try to bring down the dollar amount—which, let's face it, they probably will. Agree on paydays, as well. You may prefer to have a different set-up in each household, depending on what kind of spender you are. If you can't seem to keep money in your pockets, you may do better getting paid on a different day at each house—perhaps Saturdays at your mom's and Tuesdays at your dad's, so all your cash doesn't vanish over the weekend. If you usually need bigger chunks of change for fewer things (perhaps you tend to buy one new piece of clothing at a time, or to go out on one date each week), try to get both allowances on the same day, or as close together as possible.

Getting to Work

Before you apply for a job, assess the transportation situation. If you can walk, bike, or take public transportation, great. If not, you may need your parents to take you to and from work. Make sure they know this and agree to do it. You won't have a job for long if you can't get there!

Saving Up for a Car

The ultimate freedom, if you live in a split family, may come in the form of your very own automobile — and that costs money. Saving up for a car is a goal that you can achieve through hard work over a summer or two, and it may have a dramatic effect on your quality of life. Few teens would say "no" to a car, but if you're spending half your life in transit you may be willing to work a little harder for one.

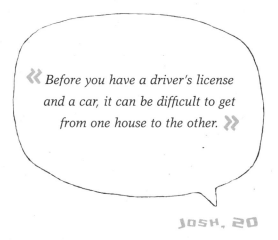

« *Before you have a driver's license and a car, it can be difficult to get from one house to the other.* »

JOSH, 20

There's no better time to bring up the subject than when you're being a mature, responsible young man or woman, trying to earn a respectable income. When you approach your parents on this subject, have a plan in place. Are you asking them if they'll allow you to buy a car? Maybe to pay for half? Do you have a particular car in mind? See the negotiation tips in Chapter 2 and go into the conversation armed with the following phrases:

"Used is fine."

"I'll pay for X, Y, and Z."

"I'd be happy to drive (insert annoying younger sibling's name here) to clarinet practice."

"I'll never ask you for anything again. Ever." (No parent will believe this one, but it's sweet to say.)

Parent Patrol

Keeping the Adults on Track

Part of the reason you feel scattered or out of control at times may simply be because your parents are not on the same page as you, your siblings, or each other. Your mom thinks some situation is one way, while your dad's understanding is totally different. For instance, maybe your mom is sure that getting you to soccer is your dad's task, while your dad is certain that it was something your mom agreed to do. That leaves you stuck without a ride—and stuck in the middle between your parents.

Everyone has different schedules, priorities, and life dramas, and this lack of unity is even further complicated if your parents are not on great speaking terms. But all hope is not lost. Even if your parents are big fans of "My house, my rules" or "Not while you're under this roof," they may still accept (and even want) some guidance from you about how to make your traveling lifestyle work. Remember, this split-up situation is not what they were planning on either, and they don't always have the answers. Mistakes will be made, and not necessarily admitted to. Try to remember that your parents are human, and give them some gentle direction when they need it.

Whose Job Is It Anyway?

You may feel like an adult—and in many ways you are—but in the end you are still living with your parents, and you rely on them for certain things. It's important that all parties know their responsibilities, and it may be up to you to get that discussion going. Talk to your parents about the things you need, and try to make some joint decisions about who is responsible for what. You can have an informal conversation, pass around an e-mail checklist, or draw up a contract that you ask them to sign. Regardless of how you approach the situation, keep track of what they have agreed to do. This way, if you are ever the recipient of "Your mother

said she was going!" or "Wasn't your father supposed to give you that?" you'll have some documentation to settle the dispute.

1. School and after school

A lot of routine things come up during the school year that require the involvement of one or both of your parents. These basic responsibilities should be sorted out between the three of you, so you know who goes to what meetings, who signs your report cards, and who does whatever else needs to be done. It's possible that your parents may decide to share some of the tasks listed below; it's possible each parent will take on sole responsibility for certain tasks. Either way, you all need to know that everything is covered—and who is responsible for what.

Ask your parents:

Who goes to parent-teacher conferences?

Who goes to/takes you to school functions (plays, concerts, etc.)?

Who signs your report card?

Who attends your games, matches, meets, and ceremonies?

Who takes you to practices, work, and other after-school obligations?

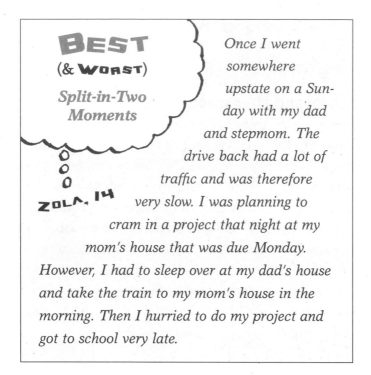

BEST
(& WORST)

Split-in-Two
Moments

Once I went somewhere upstate on a Sunday with my dad and stepmom. The drive back had a lot of traffic and was therefore very slow. I was planning to cram in a project that night at my mom's house that was due Monday. However, I had to sleep over at my dad's house and take the train to my mom's house in the morning. Then I hurried to do my project and got to school very late.

ZOLA, 14

2. Money

This is one of the biggest things married couples argue over, and that often doesn't change when they split up. Of course, your parents might be the smoothest deal-makers ever and split everything right down the middle. Or not. If they are not so great with money matters, it can help to have a discussion with them about this stuff to make it clear whom you should be relying on for what. If a discussion is out of the question, consider sending around a spreadsheet in an e-mail.

Ask your parents:

Who pays for sports uniforms?

Who pays for school pictures?

Who pays for field trips?

Who pays for school dances (including the dress or suit)?

Who pays for school lunches?

Who pays for school clothes?

Who pays for your extracurricular activities (dance lessons, art classes, etc.)?

Who pays for your cell phone?

3. Emergencies and snafus

You and your parents may have sorted out the basic logistical stuff, but what about more stressful circumstances, like emergencies or problems at school? For these situations, you might want to have some say over who should be contacted for what. If Mom totally freaks when you have a cut on your arm, you might want to have the school call Dad when you take a volleyball to the face during gym. And if Dad will never let you out again if you get that one-time "D," put your Mom's number down when your academic teachers collect your parent/guardian info.

Look at the categories below and decide which parent you want to take care of what, and then check in with them to make sure it's cool. (For each situation that involves school, make sure your teachers have the contact info you want them to have.)

• If you get in trouble at school

• If you get hurt at school

• If you get sick at school

• If you're having problems with a class

• If you miss the bus and need a ride

• If you need a ride home from a party where everyone has been drinking

> ❰❰ *I was so proud of the way my dad handled the duties of raising children when he was single. He had to adapt quickly. He would make our lunches, cook us dinners, and help us with our homework. He wasn't the best cook, but he made some killer grilled cheeses.* ❱❱
>
> JEFF, 24

When Parents Go Astray

Their split-up can leave your parents a little off-kilter. One or both of them may be angry at the other, making it difficult for them to communicate about anything, including their children. You may even find that when they talk to you, they can't stop themselves from tossing in little digs about the other parent. Although working together at co-parenting should be their focus, they may slide at times. Here are some basic things you should request of them.

1. Say only nice things about each other

The last thing you want to hear is that your dad is always late and can't handle his responsibilities, or that your mom refuses to listen to anyone. No matter how true this may be, parent-to-parent insults have no place within your earshot. Let your mom and dad know that it bothers you to hear them say mean things about each other, and gently ask them to refrain from doing so around you.

Remember that it is probably better that your parents are divorced than stuck in an unhealthy marriage. But do not fall prey to pressure to pick a favorite.

MICA, 17

2. Don't use you as their messenger

If your parents aren't speaking to each other, they may rely on you to do their talking for them. But that is not your responsibility. And when one of them doesn't like what the other one relays through you, guess who has to deal with that? You. Whether the news is good or bad, urgent or not particularly pressing, your parents need to communicate directly with each other, and not through you. If they are struggling with this, kindly suggest that they use e-mail. For scheduling, they can always resort to a Web-based calendar system (see page 55).

3. Leave the interrogations to the cop shows

Parents are just as insecure as kids, and kids tend to find this out when their parents split up. Suddenly, you may notice that your mom or dad is barraging you with question after question about the other parent, the other parent's new spouse, the other parent's stepchild, the other parent's financial situation, the other parent's — you get the point. Plead the Fifth, and let your parents know you feel uncomfortable talking about them behind their backs.

Give it time. You'll all get used to the new situation.

EMILY, 15

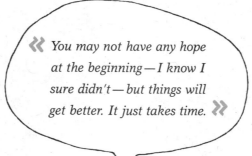

You may not have any hope at the beginning — I know I sure didn't — but things will get better. It just takes time.

SOPHIE, 17

The Golden Rules (or Lack Thereof)

One of the things that changes the most when your parents split up is the set of rules governing your existence. For some kids, this is totally annoying. It's confusing when one parent says 9 p.m. for curfew but the other says 10 p.m., or when one requires you to start homework right after school but the other one never even asks if you have homework. If you feel like you're floundering a little, try to get your parents to agree on basic rules for things like chores, homework times, curfews, and allowances, so you don't have to adjust to a new set of standards each time you switch households.

On the other hand, some teens say that the best part of having split-up parents is that you get two different sets of rules. After all, if Mom is willing to let you stay out later, you can plan to go out with that new guy or girl the next time you're at Mom's house.

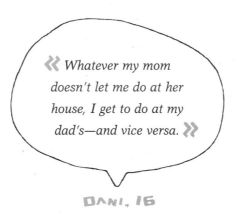

Whatever my mom doesn't let me do at her house, I get to do at my dad's—and vice versa.

DANI, 16

« At my mom's house, I am allowed to play computer games for hours, while at my dad's I have to do all my homework first. So I end up getting all my homework done at my dad's house and never finishing it at my mom's. Although I prefer to be at my mom's house, my schoolwork and grades suffer because of it. »

WESLEY, 15

Now What?

Moving Forward with Your Life

So now, you've learned some good ways to manage your day-to-day, split-living life a little better. But you know, better than anyone, that it's all easier said than done. Living in two homes will still be stressful at times even if you have the most cooperative parents in the world.

Like any difficult situation, this one calls for patience and a certain willingness to make it work. The mindset with which you approach your split-family life will be one of the main factors determining how successful it will be. Of course, even the most patient, positive person in the world can't make every situation work, so it's also possible that there will come a time when you need to ask for a change.

Look At the Bright Side

If things are working out, great. But when they're not,
you can easily get depressed about your situation. In
that mindset, you're likely to start mentally listing all of
the negative things about your circumstances. During
those moments of frustration, try making a list of all of
the beneficial things that have come about — or could
potentially come about — because your parents don't
live together.

For instance, maybe you have the opportunity to spend
more time with each parent now than you did when
they were married. Or maybe you have more independence, more peace and quiet, or great new siblings that
you wouldn't have otherwise had.

≪ *If you are in trouble with
one parent, you can always
go to the other. Also, there's
always different food in
each refrigerator.* ≫

ELI, 18

≪ *One advantage to my parents
being separated is that I get each
parent's own objective advice,
which is so much more real and
helpful when uninfluenced by
the other parent.* ≫

MAX, 16

If you're about to have a new stepparent, there could also be upsides. It might mean an extra car available to get you where you need to go, or another resource to help with your homework. If one parent is clingy and wants to know every detail of your every date, having a live-in distraction to occupy his or her time could give you more breathing room. And if your relationship with one of your parents isn't completely stellar at the moment, a new parental unit could fill the gap.

Making a list of what's good about your split-living situation is not meant to dismiss your real concerns; it's simply meant to remind you that things are not *all* bad. And everyone, in any challenging situation, needs to remind themselves of that from time to time.

> *Having two houses gives you more options. Say, for example, you really just want to have some time by yourself; you have more options and thus more chances of having an empty house. Say one house stays really cool in the summer and one really warm in the winter. Then you get the best of both worlds.* 》

JOSH, 20

Requesting a Change

If you've done all that you can do to make the situation work and are still feeling unhappy, you may want to re-examine your living situation. Not every custody arrangement will succeed. People change, households change, parents move. And sometimes, the situation never really works in the first place. Perhaps too much traveling back and forth interferes with your schedule or social life. Or, if you change households weekly, you may miss your other parent when you're away for so long. Or maybe you don't like the shuffle at all and believe it's in your best interest to sleep solely at one house and only have day visits with the other parent.

《 *Now that I'm out of high school and living full-time with my dad — instead of switching houses every other day like I did before — it's a lot easier. I talk to both parents every day on the phone and tell them what I am doing, and as long as I spend a few hours with them once a week, they are fine.* 》

KELSEY, 19

If you decide to approach your parents about a change, be clear on what's not working — and offer up solutions. It might help to go back to Chapter 1 and revisit the various living arrangements to see which ones you think might work better for you than your current situation, and to look at the negotiation skills in Chapter 2.

Custody arrangements can change — it happens all the time. But don't expect it to happen overnight. If your parents do agree to adopt a new plan, it may take them a little time to sort out the details and mesh the new arrangement with their lives. Also consider trying a temporary change — for one month, perhaps — to determine if a different arrangement really is the answer. After a month, you may decide that you liked things better the way they were.

❮❮ *It takes time to get used to such a change, and even though it may be rough in the beginning, it gets easier. You get into a routine and you stick with it. Just hang in there and know that, sooner or later, you will feel happier and stronger.* ❯❯

AMANDA, 16

Life Goes On

You may remain in the same living situation until you graduate from high school, or your arrangements may alter several times over the years. Either way, you'll find your own methods for dealing with the chaos — and may even learn to like it. Kids from split families often become more adventurous, independent, and adaptable adults. And while your life might feel like a bit of a struggle now, those qualities will be really valuable later on.

In the meantime, work toward making the situation as good as it can possibly be. And when all else fails, remember: You won't be living at home forever!

> ❮❮ *I used to wish that my parents had just stayed together until I moved away for college, so I could have skipped all the pain I experienced through middle school and high school. But then I realized that if they had stayed together for my sake, my high school home life would have been a lie. Now that I am older, I am grateful my parents got divorced. Getting a divorce allowed them to live happier lives.* ❯❯

JEFF, 24

 **Karen Buscemi** has written about beauty, fashion, health, and fitness for many magazines, including *Figure, Self, Successful Living,* and *Women's Health*. Her monthly column, "Caught Without a Catchphrase," appears in *Strut* magazine, which is distributed in *The Detroit News* and *Detroit Free Press*. She lives in Royal Oak, Michigan, with her husband and two sons.

Corinne Mucha is the author and illustrator of the Xeric Award-winning book, *My Alaskan Summer*. She grew up in southern New Jersey and attended the Rhode Island School of Design, where she graduated with a BFA in Illustration. She now lives and works in Chicago. You can find more of her comics at *www.maidenhousefly.com*.

Author Acknowledgments

Wondrous amounts of thanks to my husband, Frank Buscemi, my sons Noah Correll (my shuffler!) and Jesse Buscemi, and my mom, Margaret Shulzitski. I am also grateful to the teens and former teens from split families who contributed their stories and advice to the book, as well as to all the great people at Zest Books — especially Hallie Warshaw and my wonderful editor, Karen Macklin, whose enthusiasm and creative ideas kept me inspired and challenged me to make this book everything it could be.